CROCHET
Broomstick Lace Made Easy™

Contents

Lace Block 2	Pineapple Doily 13
Dishcloth 4	Camisole Pot Holder 16
Hot Pad 5	Bloomers Pot Holder 18
Coasters 6	Shawl 20
Place Mat 8	Scarf 22
Casserole Cover 10	Stitch Guide 24
Table Runner 12	

Introduction

Broomstick lace (also called jiffy lace and peacock's eye crochet) is a beautiful, lacy, easy-to-do technique that will add an exciting new dimension to your crochet. It is worked with a crochet hook and a broomstick lace needle (BLN), which looks like a large plastic knitting needle (in fact knitting needles can be used for this technique). You can also use a dowel rod, or even a real broomstick (which is where the name came from), although a broomstick lace needle is lighter and much easier to work with. Traditionally used for afghans and shawls, it can also be used to create beautiful clothing and fun and unique home decor items.

The process of working broomstick lace is fairly simple: In a chain or foundation row, you will pull up a long loop and

place it on the broomstick lace needle. Loops are usually worked in multiples of five or six. In the second row, the loops are worked off in groups by sliding them off the broomstick lace needle onto a crochet hook and working single crochet stitches through the center of all the loops. Each finished group forms an "eye." Broomstick lace is always worked with the right side facing.

Let's get started! The first pattern is a broomstick Lace Block, which will take you step-by-step through the process. When you are finished, use the Block as a coaster or hot pad. If you are really feeling creative, make 30 blocks in your favorite colors, sew them together in six rows of five blocks each and you have a charming and unique broomstick lace afghan. ❏❏

Many of the products used in this pattern book can be purchased from local craft, fabric and variety stores, or from the Annie's Attic Needlecraft Catalog *(see Customer Service information on page 23).*

Lace Block

Design by Ann White

SKILL LEVEL

EASY

FINISHED SIZE

6 inches square

MATERIALS

- Medium (worsted) weight cotton yarn:
  1 oz/50 yds/28g green
  ½ oz/25 yds/14g pink
- Size G/6/4mm crochet hook or size needed to obtain gauge
- Size 50 broomstick lace needle

GAUGE

9 sc = 2 inches

INSTRUCTIONS

BLOCK

Row 1: With green, ch 25, **do not turn,** slip last lp on hook onto broomstick, working left to right, back towards slip knot, [insert hook in next ch, yo, pull lp through ch and slip onto broomstick *(see Fig. 1)*] across, **do not turn,**

Row 2: Slip first 5 lps from broomstick onto hook, yo, pull lp through all 5 lps on hook *(see Fig. 2)*, ch 1, 5 sc *(see Fig. 3)* in same 5-lp group, [slip next 5 lps from broomstick onto hook, yo, pull lp through 5 lps on hook, yo, pull through 2 lps on hook *(sc made)*, 4 sc in same 5-lp group] across, **do not turn.** (25 sc)

Rows 3: Slip last lp on hook onto broomstick, working this row in **back lps** *(see Stitch Guide)*, sk first st, [insert hook in next sc, yo, pull lp through st and slip onto broomstick] across, **do not turn.**

Rows 4: Slip first 5 lps from broomstick onto hook, yo, pull lp through all 5 lps on hook, ch 1, 5 sc in same 5-lp group, [slip next 5 lps from broomstick onto hook, yo, pull lp through 5 lps on hook, yo, pull through 2 lps on hook *(sc made)*, 4 sc in same 5-lp group] across, **do not turn.**

Rows 5-8: [Rep rows 3 and 4] twice. Fasten off at end of last row.

EDGING

Join pink with sc in back lp of first st, 2 sc in same st, sc in back lp of each st across with 3 sc in back lp of last st, working in ends of rows, 4 sc around end 2 strands of each row across, working in starting ch on opposite side of row 1, 3 sc in first sc, sc in each ch across with 3 sc in last ch, working in ends of rows, 4 sc around end 2 strands of each row across, join with sl st in beg sc. Fasten off.

Fig. 1

Fig. 2
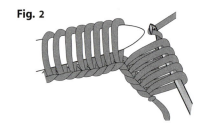

Fig. 3
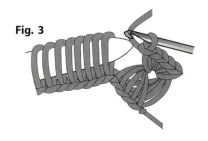

Tips

Remove the hook from the work after each long loop is placed on the BLN; reinsert it in the next chain, the back loop of next single crochet, or wherever the directions indicate.

Always twist loops in the same direction when taking them off the BLN.

Remember to always chain 1 before working single crochet in the first set of loops removed from the BLN.

Experiment with different ways of holding the BLN; some prefer to hold it under their left arm, some hold it between their thighs. Some crocheters prefer to place a small, soft pillow in their laps to rest the BLN on. Use whichever holding method is most comfortable to you.

Usually, the same number of single crochet are worked over the Eye as the number of loops it contains. For example if the Eye has 6 loops, work 6 single crochet in it. This will keep the same number of stitches in each row so the edges of the item remain straight and even. The exceptions to this rule would be working off individual Eyes, and patterns that instruct you to work more or less single crochet into the loops as a method of increasing or decreasing.

Remember that Broomstick Lace is worked with the right side facing, so don't turn at the end of the row. All loop rows are worked from left to right, and the single crochet rows are worked from right to left.

Remember that the loop on the BLN at the beginning of the loop row counts as the first loop; do not pull up a loop in the first stitch or your stitch count will be off.

Placing the first loop on the BLN

Removing the hook from the loop and placing it through the next chain

BLN with 25 loops on it

Inserting the hook under the first 5 loops

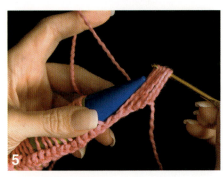

Slipping loops off BLN

Allow loops to twist

Work ch-1

Working sc's over loops

Finished Row with 5 Eyes

Pulling up lps on next row and placing BLN

Edging worked in 2 strands of loop row

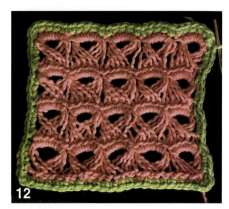

Finished block

Dishcloth

Design by Ann White

SKILL LEVEL

EASY

FINISHED SIZE
10 x 10½ inches

MATERIALS
- Medium (worsted) weight cotton yarn:
  3 oz/150 yds/85g pink
  1 oz/50 yds/28g yellow
- Size G/6/4mm crochet hook or size needed to obtain gauge
- Size 50 broomstick lace needle

GAUGE
4 sc = 1 inch

INSTRUCTIONS
DISHCLOTH

Row 1: With pink, ch 41, sc in 2nd ch from hook and in each ch across, **do not turn.** *(40 sc)*

Rows 2–9: Working left to right, slip last lp on hook onto broomstick, working this row in **back lps** *(see Stitch Guide)*, sk first st, [insert hook in next sc, yo, pull lp through st and slip onto broomstick *(see Fig. 1)*] across, **do not turn,** slip first 5 lps from broomstick onto hook, yo, pull lp through all 5 lps on hook *(see Fig. 2)*, ch 1, 5 sc in same 5-lp group *(see Fig. 3)*, [slip next 5 lps from broomstick onto hook, yo, pull lp through 5 lps on hook, yo, pull through 2 lps on hook *(sc made)*, 4 sc in same 5-lp group] across, **do not turn.** Fasten off at end of last row.

EDGING
Join yellow with sc in back lp of first st on right-hand side, sc in back lp of each st across, sc in end of each sc and 5 dc around 5 strands at end of each row across, working in starting ch on opposite side of row 1, sc in each ch across, sc in end of each sc and 5 dc around 5 strands at end of each row across, join with sl st in beg sc. Fasten off. ❑❑

Fig. 1

Fig. 2

Fig. 3
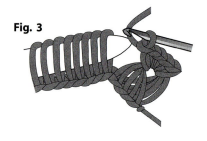

Broomstick Lace

Hot Pad

Design by Ann White

SKILL LEVEL
EASY

FINISHED SIZE
9¾ inches across

MATERIALS
- Medium (worsted) weight cotton yarn:
  1 oz/50 yds/28g each pink, yellow and green
  ½ oz/25 yds/14g purple
- Size G/6/4mm crochet hook or size needed to obtain gauge
- Size 50 broomstick lace needle

GAUGE
Rnd 1 = 2 inches across

PATTERN NOTE
Join with a slip stitch unless otherwise stated.

SPECIAL STITCHES
2-double crochet cluster (2-dc cl): [Yo, insert hook in ring, yo, pull lp through, yo, pull through 2 lps on hook] twice, yo, pull through all 3 lps on hook.

3-double crochet cluster (3-dc cl): [Yo, insert hook in ring, yo, pull lp through, yo, pull through 2 lps on hook] 3 times, yo, pull through all 4 lps on hook.

INSTRUCTIONS
HOT PAD
Rnd 1: With size G hook and purple, ch 6, join in beg ch to form ring, ch 2, **2-dc cl** *(see Special Stitches)* in ring, ch 3, [**3-dc cl** *(see Special Stitches)* in ring, ch 3] 5 times, join in top of beg cl. Fasten off. *(6 cls, 6 ch sps)*

Rnd 2: Join yellow in any ch sp, ch 3 *(counts as first dc)*, 3 dc in same sp, 4 dc in each ch sp around, join in 3rd ch of beg ch-3. *(24 dc)*

Rnd 3: (Ch 3, dc) in first st, dc in next st, [2 dc in next st, dc in next st] around, join in 3rd ch of beg ch-3. *(36 dc)*

Rnd 4: (Ch 3, dc) in first st, dc in each of next 2 sts, [2 dc in next st, dc in each of next 2 sts] around, join in 3rd ch of beg ch-3. Fasten off. *(48 dc)*

Rnd 5: Working this rnd in **back lps** *(see Stitch Guide)*, with pink, ch-2, join with sl st in first st, sl st in each of next 3 sts, pull up last lp and slip onto broomstick *(see Fig. 1)*, working from left to right and in back lps of sl sts just made, sk first st, [insert hook into next st, yo, pull lp through st and slip onto broomstick] 3 times, [insert hook into next ch of next ch-2, yo, pull lp through ch and slip onto broomstick] twice, **do not turn,** slip 6 lps from broomstick onto hook, yo, pull lp through all 6 lps on hook *(see Fig. 2)*, ch 1, 8 sc *(see Fig. 3)* in same 6-lp group, *ch 2, sl st in each of next 4 sts on last rnd, pull up last lp and slip onto broomstick, working left to right through back lps of sl sts just made, sk first st, [yo, pull lp through next st and slip onto broomstick] 3 times, [insert hook

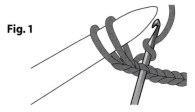
Fig. 1

Fig. 2

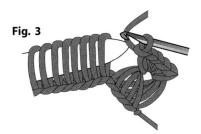
Fig. 3

Broomstick Lace

into next ch of next ch-2, yo, pull lp through ch and slip onto broomstick] twice, **do not turn,** slip 6 lps from broomstick onto hook, yo, pull lp through all 6 lps on hook, ch 1, 8 sc in same 6-lp group, rep from * around, join in beg ch of first ch-2. Fasten off. *(12 8-sc groups)*

Rnd 6: Join green in 4th st of any 8-sc group, ch 8, [sc in 4th st of next 8-sc group, ch 8] around, join in beg sc. *(12 ch sps)*

Rnd 7: Sl st in first ch sp, ch 1, (5 sc, ch 3, 5 sc) in same sp and in each ch sp around, join in beg sc. Fasten off.

Coasters

Designs by Ann White

SKILL LEVEL

EASY

FINISHED SIZE
4½ inches across

MATERIALS
- Medium (worsted) weight cotton yarn: 2 oz/100 yds/57g yellow
  1 oz/50 yds/28g each light pink, hot pink and purple
- Size G/6/4mm crochet hook or size needed to obtain gauge
- Size 50 broomstick lace needle

GAUGE
Rnds 1–3 = 2 inches across

INSTRUCTIONS
FIRST COASTER
Rnd 1: With yellow, ch 4, sl st in beg ch to form ring, ch 1, 10 sc in ring, join with sl st in beg sc. *(10 sc)*

Rnd 2: Ch 1, 2 sc in each st around, join with sl st in beg sc. *(20 sc)*

Rnd 3: Ch 1, sc in first st, 2 sc in next st, [sc in next st, 2 sc in next st] around, join with sl st in beg sc. Fasten off. *(30 sc)*

Rnd 4: Working this rnd in **back lps** *(see Stitch Guide),* join hot pink with sl st in first st, sl st in each of next 4 sts, pull up last lp and slip onto broomstick, working from left to right and in back lps of sl sts just made, sk first st, [yo, pull lp through next st and slip onto broomstick *(see Fig. 1)*] 4 times, **do not turn,** slip 5 lps from broomstick onto hook, yo, pull lp through all 5 lps on hook *(see Fig. 2),* ch 1, 8 sc *(see Fig. 3)* in same 5-lp group, sl st in last worked st on last rnd, *sl st in each of next 5 sts on last rnd, pull up last lp and slip onto broomstick, working left to right through back lps of sl sts just made, sk first st, [yo, pull lp through next st and slip onto broomstick] 4 times, **do not turn,** slip 5 lps from

6 Broomstick Lace Made Easy • Annie's Attic • Berne, IN 46711 • AnniesAttic.com

broomstick onto hook, yo, pull lp through all 5 lps on hook, ch 1, 8 sc in same 5-lp group, sl st in last worked st on last rnd, rep from * around, join with sl st in beg sl st. Fasten off.

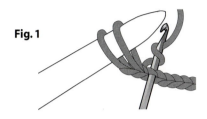
Fig. 1

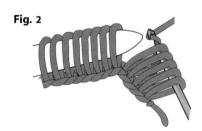
Fig. 2

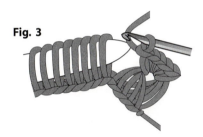
Fig. 3

Broomstick Lace

Coaster worked to point of pulling up loops

2ND COASTER

Rnd 1: With light pink, ch 4, sl st in beg ch to form ring, ch 1, 10 sc in ring, join with sl st in beg sc. Fasten off. *(10 sc)*

Rnd 2: Working this rnd in back lps, join yellow with sc in first st, sc in same st, 2 sc in each st around, join with sl st in beg sc. *(20 sc)*

Rnd 3: Ch 1, sc in first st, 2 sc in next st, [sc in next st, 2 sc in next st] around, join with sl st in beg sc. Fasten off. *(30 sc)*

Rnd 4: Working this rnd in back lps, join purple with sl st in first st, sl st in each of next 4 sts, pull up last lp and slip onto broomstick, working from left to right and in back lps of sl sts just made, sk first st, [yo, pull lp through next st and slip onto broomstick *(see Fig. 1)*] 4 times, **do not turn,** slip 5 lps from broomstick onto hook, yo, pull lp through all 5 lps on hook *(see Fig. 2),* ch 1, 8 sc *(see Fig. 3)* in same 5-lp group, sl st in last worked st on last rnd, *sl st in each of next 5 sts on last rnd, pull up last lp and slip onto broomstick, working left to right through back lps of sl sts just made, sk first st, [yo, pull lp through next st and slip onto broomstick] 4 times, **do not turn,** slip 5 lps from broomstick onto hook, yo, pull lp through all 5 lps on hook, ch 1, 8 sc in same 5-lp group, sl st in last worked st on last rnd, rep from * around, join with sl st in beg sl st. Fasten off.

3RD COASTER

Rnd 1: With purple, ch 4, sl st in beg ch to form ring, ch 1, 10 sc in ring, join with sl st in beg sc. Fasten off. *(10 sc)*

Rnd 2: Working this rnd in back lps, join yellow with sc in first st, sc in same st, 2 sc in each st around, join with sl st in beg sc. *(20 sc)*

Rnd 3: Ch 1, sc in first st, 2 sc in next st, [sc in next st, 2 sc in next st] around, join with sl st in beg sc. Fasten off. *(30 sc)*

Rnd 4: Working this rnd in back lps, join pink with sl st in first st, sl st in each of next 4 sts, pull up last lp and slip onto broomstick, working from left to right and in back lps of sl sts just made, sk first st, [yo, pull lp through next st and slip onto broomstick *(see Fig. 1)*] 4 times, **do not turn,** slip 5 lps from broomstick onto hook, yo, pull lp through all 5 lps on hook *(see Fig. 2),* ch 1, 8 sc *(see Fig. 3)* in same 5-lp group, sl st in last worked st on last rnd, *sl st in each of next 5 sts on last rnd, pull up last lp and slip onto broomstick, working left to right through back lps of sl sts just made, sk first st, [yo, pull lp through next st and slip onto broomstick] 4 times, **do not turn,** slip 5 lps from broomstick onto hook, yo, pull lp through all 5 lps on hook, ch 1, 8 sc in same 5-lp group, sl st in last worked st on last rnd, rep from * around, join with sl st in beg sl st. Fasten off. ❑❑

Place Mat

Design by Ann White

SKILL LEVEL
■■□□ EASY

FINISHED SIZE
11 x 16 inches

MATERIALS
- Bernat Cottontots medium (worsted) weight cotton yarn (3½ oz/171 yds/100g per skein):
    1 skein each #90712 lime berry and #90616 lemon berry
- Size G/6/4mm crochet hook or size needed to obtain gauge
- Size 50 broomstick lace needle

GAUGE
9 sc = 2 inches

INSTRUCTIONS
PLACE MAT

Row 1: With lime berry, ch 21, sc in 2nd ch from hook and in each ch across, **do not turn.** *(20 sc)*

Row 2: Working this row in **back lps** *(see Stitch Guide)*, pull up last lp and slip onto broomstick, working left to right, sk first st [insert hook in next st, yo, pull lp through st and slip onto broomstick *(see Fig. 1)*] across, **do not turn,** slip first 5 lps from broomstick onto hook, yo, pull lp through all 5 lps on hook *(see Fig. 2)*, ch 1, 5 sc *(see Fig. 3)* in same 5-lp group, [slip next 5 lps from broomstick onto hook, yo, pull lp through 5 lps on hook, yo, pull through 2 lps on hook *(sc made)*, 4 sc in same 5-lp group] across, **do not turn.** *(20 sc)*

Row 3: For **beg inc,** ch 5, pull up last lp and slip on broomstick, working left to right in chs and back lps of sts, [insert hook in next ch or st, yo, pull lp through ch or st and slip onto broomstick] across, for **end inc,** sl st in front lp of last st, ch 6, sc in 2nd ch from hook and in each of next 4 chs, pull up lp on hook and place on broomstick, sk first sl st, [insert hook in next sl st, yo, pull lp through st and slip onto broomstick] across, **do not turn,** slip first 5 lps from broomstick onto hook, yo, pull lp through all 5 lps on hook, ch 1, 5 sc in same 5-lp group, [slip next 5 lps from broomstick onto hook, yo, pull lp through 5 lps on hook, yo, pull through 2 lps on hook *(sc made)*, 4 sc in same 5-lp group] across, **do not turn.** *(30 sc)*

Row 4: Rep row 3. Fasten off. *(40 sc)*

Row 5: Join lemon berry with sl st in last st, rep row 3. *(50 sc)*

Increasing on the left side

Increasing on the right side

Rows 6–10: Working this row in back lps, pull up last lp and slip onto broomstick, working left to right, sk first st, [insert hook in next st, yo, pull lp through st and slip onto broomstick] across, **do not turn,** slip first 5 lps from broomstick onto hook, yo, pull lp through all 5 lps on hook, ch 1, 5 sc in same 5-lp group, [slip next 5 lps from broomstick onto hook, yo, pull lp through 5 lps on hook, yo, pull through 2 lps on hook *(sc made)*, 4 sc in same 5-lp group] across, **do not turn.** Fasten off at end of last row.

Row 11: Working this row in back lps, for **beg dec,** sk last 5 sts of left-hand side, join lime berry with sl st in next st, pull up lp and slip onto broomstick, [insert hook in next st, yo, pull lp through st and slip onto broomstick] across, leaving last 5 sts unworked for **end dec, do not turn,** slip first 5 lps from broomstick onto hook, yo, pull lp through all 5 lps on hook, ch 1, 5 sc in same 5-lp group, [slip next 5 lps from broomstick onto hook, yo, pull lp through 5 lps on hook, yo, pull through 2 lps on hook *(sc made)*, 4 sc in same 5-lp group] across, **do not turn.** Fasten off. *(40 sc)*

Rows 12 & 13: Rep row 11.

Row 14: Join lime berry with sl st in first st on right-hand side, sl st in each st across. Fasten off. ❏❏

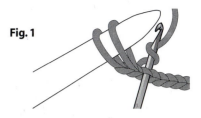
Fig. 1

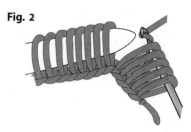
Fig. 2

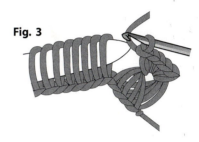
Fig. 3

Broomstick Lace

Casserole Cover

Design by Ann White

SKILL LEVEL
■■□□ EASY

FINISHED SIZE
Fits 2-quart round casserole dish

MATERIALS
- Medium (worsted) weight cotton yarn: 4 oz/200 yds/114g purple; 2 oz/100 yds/56g yellow
- Size G/6/4mm crochet hook or size needed to obtain gauge
- Size 50 broomstick lace needle
- 11 stitch holders

GAUGE
4 dc = 1 inch; 5 dc rows = 3 inches

PATTERN NOTE
Join with a slip stitch unless otherwise stated.

SPECIAL STITCH
Cluster (cl): *Yo twice, insert hook in 4th ch from hook, yo, pull lp through, [yo, pull through 2 lps on hook] twice, rep from *, yo, pull through all 3 lps on hook.

INSTRUCTIONS
CASSEROLE COVER
Rnd 1: With purple, ch 4, 11 dc in 4th ch from hook, join in 3rd ch of beg ch-3. *(12 dc)*

Rnd 2: Ch 3 *(counts as first dc)*, dc in same st, 2 dc in each st around, join in 3rd ch of beg ch-3. *(24 dc)*

Rnd 3: (Ch 3, dc) in first st, dc in next st, [2 dc in next st, dc in next st] around, join in 3rd ch of beg ch-3. *(36 dc)*

Rnd 4: (Ch 3, dc) in first st, dc in each of next 2 sts, [2 dc in next st, dc in each of next 2 sts] around, join in 3rd ch of beg ch-3. *(48 dc)*

Rnd 5: (Ch 3, dc) in first st, dc in each of next 3 sts, [2 dc in next st, dc in each of next 3 sts] around, join in 3rd ch of beg ch-3. *(60 dc)*

Rnd 6: (Ch 3, dc) in first st, dc in each of next 4 sts, [2 dc in next st, dc in each of next 4 sts] around, join in 3rd ch of beg ch-3. *(72 dc)*

Rnd 7: Working this rnd in **back lps** *(see Stitch Guide)*, ch 3, dc in each st around, join in 3rd ch of beg ch-3.

Rnd 8: Ch 3, dc in each st around, join in 3rd ch of beg ch-3. Fasten off.

Rnd 9: Join yellow with sc in first st, sc in each st around, join in back lp of beg sc. *(72 sc)*

Rnd 10: Working this rnd in back lps, pull up last lp and slip onto broomstick *(see Fig. 1)*, working from left to right, sk first st, [insert hook into next st, yo, pull lp through st and slip onto broomstick] 5 times, slide lps off broomstick onto a st holder, *[insert hook in next st, yo, pull lp through st and slip onto broomstick] 6 times, slide lps off broomstick onto a st holder, rep from * 9 times, [insert hook in next st, yo, pull lp through st and slip onto broomstick] 6 times, **do not turn**, slip 6 lps from broomstick onto hook, yo, pull lp through all 6 lps on hook *(see Fig. 2)*, ch 1, 6 sc *(see Fig. 3)* in same 6-lp group, ch 2, [insert hook in next 6 lps on next holder, remove holder, yo, pull through 6 lps on hook, yo, pull through 2 lps on hook *(sc made)*, 5 sc in same 6-lp group, ch 2] around, join in beg sc. Fasten off. *(72 sc, 12 ch sps)*

Rnd 11: Join purple in first st, ch 3, dc in each st and 2 dc in each ch sp around, join in 3rd ch of beg ch-3. *(96 dc)*

FIRST STRAP

Row 1: Now working in rows, ch 2 *(is not used or counted as a st)*, dc in each of next 13 sts, **dc dec** *(see Stitch Guide)* in next 2 sts, leaving rem sts unworked, turn. *(14 dc)*

Row 2: Ch 2, dc in each of next 11 sts, dc dec in last 2 sts, turn. *(12 dc)*

Row 3: Ch 2, dc in each of next 9 sts, dc dec in last 2 sts, turn. *(10 dc)*

Row 4: Ch 2, dc in each of next 7 sts, dc dec in last 2 sts, turn. *(8 dc)*

Rows 5–8: Ch 3, dc in each st across, turn.

Row 9: Ch 2, 2 dc in next st, ch 4, **cl** *(see Special Stitch)* in 4th ch from hook, sk next 4 sts on last row, dc dec in last 2 sts. Fasten off.

2ND STRAP

Row 1: Join purple in next unworked st on rnd 11 of Cover, ch 2, dc in each of next 13 sts, dc dec in next 2 sts, leaving rem sts unworked, turn. *(14 dc)*

Rows 2–9: Rep rows 2–9 of First Strap.

3RD STRAP

Row 1: Sk next 16 sts on row 11 of Cover, join purple in next st, ch 2, dc in each of next 13 sts, dc dec in next 2 sts, leaving rem sts unworked, turn. *(14 dc)*

Rows 2–9: Rep rows 2–9 of First Strap.

4TH STRAP

Row 1: Join purple in next unworked st on rnd 11 of Cover, ch 2, dc in each of next 13 sts, dc dec in next 2 sts, leaving last 16 sts unworked, turn. *(14 dc)*

Rows 2–9: Rep rows 2–9 of First Strap.

EDGING

Join yellow with sc in any st, evenly spacing sts so piece lies flat, sc around entire outside edge, join in beg sc. Fasten off. ❑❑

Fig. 1

Fig. 2

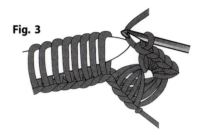

Fig. 3

Broomstick Lace

Holding base of loops

Table Runner

Design by Ann White

SKILL LEVEL
EASY

FINISHED SIZE
13 x 25 inches, excluding Fringe

MATERIALS
- Bernat Cottontots medium (worsted) weight cotton yarn (3½ oz/171 yds/100g per skein):
  - 2 skeins #90616 lemon berry
  - 1 skein each #90712 lime berry, #90421 strawberry and #90321 grape berry
- Size G/6/4mm crochet hook or size needed to obtain gauge
- Size 50 broomstick lace needle

GAUGE
4 sc = 1 inch

INSTRUCTIONS
TABLE RUNNER

Row 1: With lemon berry, ch 101, sc in 2nd ch from hook and in each ch across, **do not turn.** (100 sc)

Row 2: Working this row in **back lps** *(see Stitch Guide)*, pull up lp on hook and slip onto broomstick, working left to right, sk first st, [insert hook in next st, yo, pull lp through st and slip onto broomstick *(see Fig. 1)*] across, **do not turn,** slip first 5 lps from broomstick onto hook, yo, pull lp through all 5 lps on hook *(see Fig. 2)*, ch 1, 5 sc *(see Fig. 3)* in same 5-lp group, [slip next 5 lps from broomstick onto hook, yo, pull lp through 5 lps on hook, yo, pull through 2 lps on hook *(sc made)*, 4 sc in same 5-lp group] across, **change color** *(see Stitch Guide)* to strawberry in last st made, **do not turn.** (100 sc)

Rows 3: Slip last lp on hook onto broomstick, working this row in back lps, sk first st, [insert hook in next sc, yo, pull lp through st and slip onto broomstick] across, **do not turn,** slip first 5 lps from broomstick onto hook, yo, pull lp through all 5 lps on hook, ch 1, 5 sc in same 5-lp group, [slip next 5 lps from broomstick onto hook, yo, pull lp through 5 lps on hook, yo, pull through 2 lps on hook *(sc made)*, 4 sc in same 5-lp group] across, changing to lemon berry in last st made, **do not turn.**

Row 4: Rep row 3, changing to grape berry in last st made.

Row 5: Rep row 3.

Row 6: Rep row 3, changing to lime berry in last st made.

Row 7: Rep row 3.

Row 8: Rep row 3, changing to grape berry in last st made.

Row 9: Rep row 3.

Row 10: Rep row 3, changing to strawberry in last st made.
Row 11: Rep row 3.
Row 12: Rep row 3, do not change colors. Fasten off.

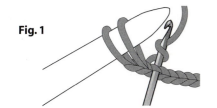
Fig. 1

FRINGE
Cut 6 strands yarn, each 16 inches long. With all strands held tog, fold in half, insert hook through 5 strands at end of broomstick row, pull fold through, pull all loose strands through fold; tighten. Trim.

Matching row colors, Fringe in each end of each broomstick lace row. ❑❑

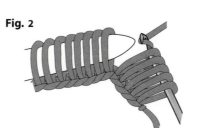
Fig. 2

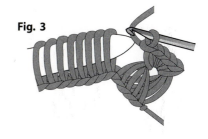
Fig. 3

Broomstick Lace

Pineapple Doily

Design by Darla Hassell

SKILL LEVEL

EASY

FINISHED SIZE
14½ inches in diameter

MATERIALS
- Aunt Lydia's Classic size 10 crochet cotton (350 yds per ball): 1 ball each #422 golden yellow, #119 violet and #131 fudge brown
- Size 3 crochet cotton: 12 inches orange
- Size 7/1.65mm steel crochet hook or size needed to obtain gauge
- Sizes 13 and 19 knitting needles
- 39 stitch holders

GAUGE
Rnd 1 = 1½ inches across

PATTERN NOTE
Join with a slip stitch unless otherwise stated.

INSTRUCTIONS
DOILY
Rnd 1: With golden yellow, ch 19, join in beg ch to form ring, ch 4 *(counts as first tr)*, 39 tr in ring, join in 4th ch of beg ch-4. *(40 tr)*

Rnd 2: Ch 1, sc in first st, [ch 3, sk next st, sc in next st] around to last st, ch 2, sk last st, join with sc in beg sc. *(20 ch sps)*

Rnd 3: Ch 1, sc around joining sc, [ch 4, sc in next ch sp] around, ch 2, join with dc in beg sc.

Rnd 4: Ch 1, sc around joining dc, [ch 5, sc in next ch sp] around, ch 3, join with dc in beg sc.

Rnd 5: Ch 1, sc around joining dc, [ch 6, sc in next ch sp] around, ch 3, join with tr in beg sc.

Rnd 6: Ch 1, sc around joining tr, [ch 7, sc in next ch sp] around, ch 4, join with tr in beg sc.

Rnd 7: Ch 1, sc around joining tr, ch 8, [sc in next ch sp, ch 8] around, join in beg sc. Fasten off.

Rnd 8: Join fudge brown in any ch sp, ch 3 *(counts as first dc)*, dc in same ch sp, ch 8, [2 dc in next ch sp, ch 8] around, join in 3rd ch of beg ch-3. *(40 dc, 20 ch sps)*

Rnd 9: Sl st in next st, sl st in next ch sp, ch 3, 9 dc in same sp, 10 dc in each ch sp around, join in 3rd ch of beg ch-3. Fasten off. *(200 dc)*

Rnd 10: With violet, pull up lp in last st and slip onto size 19 knitting needles *(see Fig. 1)*, working from left to right, sk first st, [insert hook into next st, yo, pull lp through st and slip onto needle] 4 times, slide lps off needle onto a st holder, *[insert

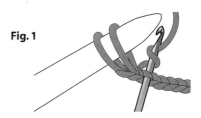
Fig. 1

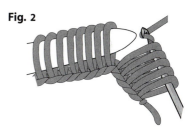
Fig. 2

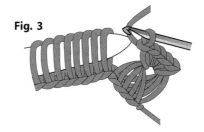
Fig. 3

Broomstick Lace

hook in next st, yo, pull lp through st and slip onto needle] 5 times, slide lps off needles onto a st holder, rep from * 37 times, [insert hook in next st, yo, pull lp through st and slip onto needle] 5 times, **do not turn,** slip 5 lps from needle onto hook, yo, pull

lp through all 5 lps on hook *(see Fig. 2)*, ch 1, 5 sc *(see Fig. 3)* in same 5-lp group, ch 1, [insert hook in next 5 lps on next holder, remove holder, yo, pull through 5 lps on hook, yo, pull through 2 lps on hook *(sc made)*, 4 sc in same 5-lp group, ch 1] around, join in beg sc. Fasten off. *(40 5-sc groups, 40 ch-1 sps)*

Rnd 11: Join fudge brown with sc in center st of any 5-sc group, ch 6, [sc in center st of next 5-sc group, ch 6] around, join in beg sc. *(40 sc, 40 ch sps)*

Rnd 12: (Sl st, ch 3, 5 dc) in next ch sp, 6 dc in each ch sp around, join in 3rd ch of beg ch-3. Fasten off. *(40 6-dc groups)*

Rnd 13: Join golden yellow in first st of any 6-dc group, (ch 3, dc) in same st, *ch 3, (2 dc, ch 2, 2 dc) in first st of next 6-dc group, ch 3, 2 dc in first st of next 6-dc group, ch 5, (dc, ch 2, dc) in first st of next 6-dc group, ch 8, sk next 6-dc group, (2 dc, ch 2, 2 dc) in first st of next 6-dc group, ch 8, sk next 6-dc group, (dc, ch 3, dc) in first st of next 6-dc group, ch 5**, 2 dc in first st of next 6-dc group, rep from * around, ending last rep at **, join in 3rd ch of beg ch-3. *(80 dc, 20 ch-2 sps, 10 ch-8 sps, 10 ch-5 sps, 10 ch-3 sps)*

Rnd 14: (Sl st, ch 3, dc) in next st, *ch 3, sk next ch sp, 7 dc in next ch-2 sp, ch 3, sk next ch sp, 2 dc in

2nd st of next 2-dc group, ch 5, sk next ch sp, (dc, ch 2, dc) in next ch sp, ch 8, sk next ch sp, (2 dc, ch 2, 2 dc) in next ch sp, ch 8, sk next ch sp, (dc, ch 2, dc) in next ch sp, ch 5, sk next ch sp**, 2 dc in 2nd st of next 2-dc group, rep from * around, ending last rep at **, join in 3rd ch of beg ch-3. *(95 dc, 10 ch-8 sps, 10 ch-5 sps, 10 ch-3 sps)*

Row 15: (Sl st, ch 3, dc) in next st, *ch 3, sk next ch sp, dc in next dc, [ch 1, dc in next dc] 6 times, ch 3, sk next ch sp, 2 dc in 2nd st of next 2-dc group, ch 5, sk next ch sp, (dc, ch 2, dc) in next ch sp, ch 9, sk next ch sp, (2 dc, ch 2, 2 dc) in next ch sp, ch 9, sk next ch sp, (dc, ch 2, dc) in next ch sp, ch 5, sk next ch sp**, 2 dc in 2nd st of next 2-dc group, rep from * around, ending last rep at **, join in 3rd ch of beg ch-3. *(95 dc, 10 ch-9 sps, 10 ch-5 sps, 10 ch-3 sps)*

Rnd 16: (Sl st, ch 3, dc) in next st, *ch 3, sk next ch sp, sc in next ch-1 sp, [ch 3, sc in next ch-1 sp] 5 times, ch 3, sk next ch sp, 2 dc in 2nd st of next 2-dc group, ch 5, sk next ch sp, (dc, ch 2, dc) in next ch sp, ch 10, sk next ch sp, (2 dc, ch 2, dc, ch 2, 2 dc) in next ch sp, ch 10, sk next ch sp, (dc, ch 2, dc) in next ch sp, ch 5, sk next ch sp**, 2 dc in 2nd st of next 2-dc group, rep from * around, ending last rep at **, join in 3rd ch of beg ch-3. *(65 dc, 35 ch-3 sps, 30 sc, 10 ch-10 sps, 10 ch-5 sps)*

Rnd 17: (Sl st, ch 3, dc) in next st, *ch 3, sk next ch sp, sc in next ch sp, [ch 3, sc in next ch sp] 4 times, ch 3, sk next ch sp, 2 dc in 2nd st of next 2-dc group, ch 5, sk next ch sp, (dc, ch 2, dc) in next ch sp, ch 10, sk next ch sp, (2 dc, ch 2, 2 dc) in next ch sp, ch 2, (2 dc, ch 2, 2 dc) in next ch sp, ch 10, sk next ch sp, (dc, ch 2, dc) in next ch sp, ch 5, sk next ch sp**, 2 dc in 2nd st of next 2-dc group, rep from * around, ending last rep at **, join in 3rd ch of beg ch-3. *(80 dc, 30 ch-3 sps, 25 sc, 10 ch-10 sps, 10 ch-5 sps)*

Rnd 18: (Sl st, ch 3, dc) in next st, *ch 3, sk next ch sp, sc in next ch sp, [ch 3, sc in next ch sp] 3 times, ch 3, sk next ch sp, 2 dc in 2nd st of next 2-dc group, ch 5, sk next ch sp, (dc, {ch 2, dc} twice) in next ch sp, ch 8, sk next ch sp, [(2 dc, ch 2, 2 dc) in next ch sp, ch 2] twice, (2 dc, ch 2, 2 dc) in next ch sp, ch 8, sk next ch sp, (dc, {ch 2, dc} twice) in next ch sp, ch 5, sk next ch sp**, 2 dc in 2nd st of next 2-dc group, rep from * around, ending last rep at **, join in 3rd ch of beg ch-3. *(110 dc, 25 ch-3 sps, 20 sc, 10 ch-8 sps, 10 ch-5 sps)*

Rnd 19: (Sl st, ch 4, tr) in next st, *ch 4, sk next ch sp, sc in next ch sp, [ch 4, sc in next ch sp] twice, ch 4, sk next ch sp, 2 tr in 2nd st of next 2-dc group, ch 6, sk next ch sp, (dc, ch 2, dc) in next ch sp, ch 3, (dc, ch 2, dc) in next ch sp, ch 6, sk next ch sp, [(2 dc, ch 2, 2 dc) in next ch sp, ch 3, sk next ch sp] twice, (2 dc, ch 2, 2 dc) in next ch sp, ch 6, sk next ch sp, (dc, ch 2, dc) in next ch sp, ch 3, (dc, ch 2, dc) in next ch sp, ch 6, sk next ch sp**, 2 tr in 2nd st of next 2-dc group, rep from * around, ending last rep at **, join in 4th ch of beg ch-4. *(100 dc, 20 tr, 15 sc)*

Rnd 20: (Sl st, ch 4, tr) in next st, *ch 4, sk next ch sp, sc in next ch sp, ch 4, sc in next ch sp, ch 4, sk next ch sp, 2 tr in 2nd st of next 2-tr group, ch 8, sk next ch sp, (dc, ch 2, dc) in next ch sp, ch 4, sk next ch sp, (dc, ch 2, dc) in next ch sp, ch 5, sk next ch sp, [(2 dc, ch 2, 2 dc) in next ch sp, ch 4, sk next ch sp] twice, (2 dc, ch 2, 2 dc) in next ch sp, ch 5, sk next ch sp, (dc, ch 2, dc) in next ch sp, ch 4, sk next ch sp, (dc, ch 2, dc) in next ch sp, ch 8, sk next ch sp**, 2 tr in 2nd st of next 2-tr group, rep from * around, ending last rep at **, join in 4th ch of beg ch-4. *(100 dc, 20 tr, 10 sc)*

Rnd 21: (Sl st, ch 4, tr) in next st, *sk next ch sp, (tr, ch 3, tr) in next ch sp, sk next ch sp, 2 tr in 2nd st of next 2-tr group, ch 8, sk next ch sp, (dc, ch 2, dc) in next ch sp, ch 5, sk next ch sp, (dc, ch 2, dc) in next ch sp, [ch 5, sk next ch sp, (2 dc, ch 2, 2 dc) in next ch sp] 3 times, [ch 5, sk next ch sp, (dc, ch 2, dc) in next ch sp] twice, ch 8, sk next ch sp, 2 tr in 2nd st of next 2-tr group, rep from * around, ending last rep at **, join in 4th ch of beg ch-4. *(100 dc, 30 tr)*

Rnd 22: Sl st in each of next 2 sts, (sl st, ch 4, 6 tr) in next ch sp, *11 sc in next ch sp, (sc, ch 3, sc) in next ch sp, 6 sc in next ch sp, (sc, ch 3, sc) in next ch sp, 5 sc in next ch sp, sc in next dc, (sc, ch 3, sc) in next ch sp, sk next dc, sc in next dc, [6 sc in next ch sp, sc in next dc, (sc, ch 3, sc) in next ch sp, sk next dc, sc in next dc] twice, 5 sc in next ch sp, (sc, ch 3, sc) in next ch sp, 11 sc in next ch sp**, 7 tr in next ch sp, rep from * around, ending last rep at **, join in 4th ch of beg ch-4. Fasten off.

EDGING

Row 1: Join fudge brown with sc in next to last ch-3 sp, ch 9, sc in next ch-3 sp, ch 11, sc in next tr, ch 8, sk next 6 tr, sc in next sc, ch 11, sc in next ch-3 sp, ch 9, sc in next ch-3 sp, leaving rem sts unworked, turn. *(5 ch sps)*

Row 2: (Sl st, ch 3, 11 dc) in first ch sp, 12 dc in each of last 4 ch sps, turn. Fasten off. *(60 dc)*

Row 3: Join violet with sl st in next ch-3 sp on row 22, working left to right in sts on last row, [insert hook into next st, yo, pull lp through st and slip onto size 13 knitting needle] across, sl st in next ch-3 sp on row 22, **do not turn,** slip 4 lps from needle onto hook, yo, pull lp through all 4 lps on hook, ch 1, 4 sc in same 4-lp group, [ch 1, slip next 4 lps from needle onto hook, yo, pull lp through 4 lps on hook, yo, pull through 2 lps on hook *(sc made)*, 3 sc in same 4-lp group] across, sl st in next sc. Fasten off.

[Sk next 2 ch-3 sps on rnd 22, join in next ch-3 sp and work Edging] 4 times.

Tie orange yarn into a bow around one st on rnd 11.

Camisole Pot Holder

Design by Darla Hassell

SKILL LEVEL
EASY

FINISHED SIZE
8½ inches tall x 10½ inches wide

MATERIALS
- Bernat Cottontots medium (worsted) weight cotton yarn (3½ oz/171 yds/100g per skein):
  1 skein each #90005 wonder white, #90712 lime berry and #90616 lemon berry
  12 inches #90129 blue berry
- Size H/8/5mm crochet hook or size needed to obtain gauge
- Size 35 broomstick lace needle
- Tapestry needle
- 20 stitch holders

GAUGE
3 dc = 1 inch; 5 dc rows = 3 inches

PATTERN NOTE
Join with a slip stitch unless otherwise stated.

INSTRUCTIONS
CAMISOLE
Rnd 1: With wonder white, ch 36, join in beg ch to form ring, ch 3 *(counts as first dc)*, dc in each ch around, join in 3rd ch of beg ch-3. Drop lp from hook. *(36 dc)*

Rnd 2: With lemon berry, pull up lp in last st and slip onto broomstick *(see Fig. 1)*, working from left to right, sk first st, [insert hook into next st, yo, pull lp through st and slip onto broomstick] twice, slide lps off broomstick onto a st holder, *[insert hook in next st, yo, pull lp through st and slip onto broomstick] 3 times, slide lps off broomstick onto a st holder, rep from * 9 times, [insert hook in next st, yo, pull lp through st and slip onto broomstick] 3 times, **do not turn,** slip 3 lps from broomstick onto hook, yo, pull lp through all 3 lps on hook *(see Fig. 2)*, ch 1, 5 sc *(see Fig. 3)* in same 3-lp group, ch 2, [insert hook in next 3 lps on next holder, remove holder, yo, pull through 3 lps on hook, yo, pull through 2 lps on hook *(sc made)*, 4 sc in same 3-lp group, ch 2] around, join in beg sc. Fasten off. *(60 sc, 12 ch sps)*

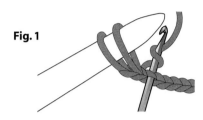

Fig. 1

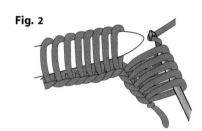

Fig. 2

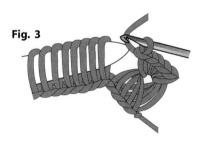

Fig. 3

Broomstick Lace

Rnd 3: Working behind last rnd, pick up dropped lp of wonder white, ch 3, dc in each of next 8 sts, ch 1, dc in each of next 18 sts, ch 1, dc in each of last 9 sts, join in 3rd ch of beg ch-3. *(36 dc, 2 ch-1 sps)*

Rnds 4–9: Ch 3, dc in each st around with (dc, ch 1, dc) in each ch-1 sp around, join in 3rd ch of beg ch-3. *(60 dc)*

Rnd 10: Ch 3, dc in each st around with 2 dc in each ch-1 sp around. *(64 dc)*

Rnd 11: With WS facing, pull up lp of lemon berry in last st and slip onto broomstick, working from left to right, sk first st, [insert hook into next st, yo, pull lp through st and slip onto broomstick] twice, slide lps off broomstick onto a st holder, *[insert hook in next st, yo, pull lp through st and slip onto broomstick] 3 times, slide lps off broomstick onto a st holder, rep from * 18 times, [insert hook in next st, yo, pull lp through st and slip onto broomstick] 3 times, leaving last st unworked, **do not turn,** slip 3 lps from broomstick onto hook, yo, pull lp through all 3 lps on hook, ch 1, 5 sc in same 3-lp group, ch 2, [insert hook in next 3 lps on next holder, remove holder, yo, pull through 3 lps on hook, yo, pull through 2 lps on hook *(sc made)*, 4 sc in same 3-lp group, ch 2] around, join in beg sc. Fasten off. *(105 sc)*

Rnd 12: With RS facing, join lime berry with sc in first st on rnd 10, ch 4, sk next st, [sc in next st, ch 4, sk next st] around, join in beg sc. Fasten off.

BOTTOM TRIM
Working in starting ch on opposite side of rnd 1, join lime berry with sc in first ch, sc in each ch around, join in beg sc. Fasten off.

STRAP
Make 2.

Row 1: With wonder white, ch 17, dc in 4th ch from hook and in each ch across, turn. *(15 dc)*

Row 2: Ch 3, dc in each st across, turn.

Row 3: Ch 1, sc in each st across, turn. Fasten off.

Row 4: Join lime berry with sc in first st, [ch 4, sk next st, sc in next st] across. Fasten off.

With last row facing out, sew 1 Strap to each side, below last rnd of Camisole on inside *(see photo)*.

Tie blue berry in bow around center front st below last rnd of Camisole. ❏❏

Bloomers Pot Holder

Design by Darla Hassell

SKILL LEVEL

■■□□ EASY

FINISHED SIZE

9 inches tall x 12 inches wide

MATERIALS
- Bernat Cottontots medium (worsted) weight cotton yarn (3½ oz/171 yds/100g per skein):
  1 skein each #90005 wonder white, #90712 lime berry and #90616 lemon berry
  12 inches #90129 blue berry
- Size H/8/5mm crochet hook or size needed to obtain gauge
- Size 19 knitting needle
- Size 35 broomstick lace needle
- Tapestry needle
- 9 stitch holders

GAUGE

3 dc = 1 inch; 5 dc rows = 3 inches

PATTERN NOTE

Join with a slip stitch unless otherwise stated.

INSTRUCTIONS

BLOOMERS

Rnd 1: With wonder white, starting at waist, ch 40, join in beg ch to form ring, ch 1, sc in each ch around, join in beg sc. *(40 sc)*

Rnd 2: Ch 3 *(counts as first dc)*, dc in each st around, join in 3rd ch of beg ch-3. *(40 dc)*

Rnd 3: Ch 3, dc in each of next 9 sts, ch 1, dc in each of next 20 sts ch 1, dc in each of last 10 sts, join in 3rd ch of beg ch-3. *(40 dc, 2 ch-1 sps)*

Rnds 4 & 5: Ch 3, dc in each st around with (dc, ch 1, dc) in each ch-1 sp, join in 3rd ch of beg ch-3. At end of last rnd, drop lp from hook. *(44 dc, 48 dc)*

Row 6: Now working in rows, for back, with lemon berry, pull up lp in 12th st to left of 2nd ch-1 sp and slip onto size 19 knitting needle *(see Fig. 1)*, working left to right, [insert hook into next st, yo, pull lp through st and slip onto needle] 23 times *(12 lps pulled up on each side of ch-1 sp)*,

do not turn, slip 3 lps from needle onto hook, yo, pull lp through all 3 lps on hook *(see Fig. 2)*, ch 1, 5 sc *(see Fig. 3)* in same 3-lp group, [ch 2, slip next 3 lps from needle onto hook, yo, pull lp through 3 lps on hook, yo, pull through 2 lps on hook *(sc made)*, 4 sc in same 3-lp group] across. Fasten off. *(8 5-sc groups)*

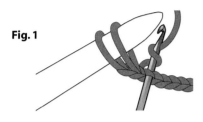

Fig. 1

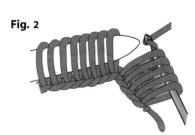

Fig. 2

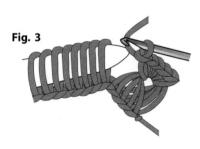

Fig. 3

Broomstick Lace

Rnd 7: Now working in rnds behind 5-sc groups, pick up dropped lp of wonder white, ch 3, dc in each st around with (dc, ch 1, dc) in each ch-1 sp, join in 3rd ch of beg ch-3. Drop lp from hook. *(52 dc)*

Row 8: Working below last set of 5-sc groups, rep row 6.

Rnd 9: Rep rnd 7. *(56 dc)*

Rnd 10: Ch 3, dc in each st around to next ch sp, (dc, ch 1, dc) in next ch sp, dc in each st around to next ch sp, dc in next ch sp, flatten Bloomers and sc in ch-1 sp on opposite side of Bloomers, dc in same ch sp on this side of Bloomers, dc in each st around, join in 3rd ch of beg ch-3. *(60 dc, 1 sc)*

FIRST LEG

Rnd 1: Ch 3, dc in each st across to next ch sp, sk next sc worked in next ch sp and next 30 dc, dc in last 15 sts, join in 3rd ch of beg ch-3. *(30 dc)*

Rnds 2–6: Ch 3, dc in each st around, join in 3rd ch of beg ch-3. Fasten off at end of last rnd.

Rnd 7: With WS facing, pull up lp of lemon berry in last st and slip onto broomstick, working from left to right, sk first st, [insert hook in next st, yo, pull lp through st and slip onto broomstick] twice, slide lps off broomstick onto a st holder, *[insert hook in next st, yo, pull lp through st and slip onto broomstick] 3 times, slide lps off broomstick onto a st holder, rep from * 7 times, [insert hook in next st, yo, pull lp through st and slip onto broomstick] 3 times, **do not turn,** slip 3 lps from broomstick onto hook, yo, pull lp through all 3 lps on hook, ch 1, 5 sc in same 3-lp group, ch 2, [insert hook in next 3 lps on next holder, remove holder, yo, pull through 3 lps on hook, yo, pull through 2 lps on hook *(sc made)*, 4 sc in same 3-lp group, ch 2] around, join in beg sc. Fasten off. *(10 5-sc groups)*

Rnd 8: With RS facing, join lime berry with sc in first st on rnd 6, ch 4, sk next st, [sc in next st, ch 4, sk next st] around, join in beg sc. Fasten off.

2ND LEG

Rnd 1: Join wonder white in first unworked dc on rnd 10 of Bloomers, ch 3, dc in each unworked dc around, join in 3rd ch of beg ch-3. *(30 dc)*

Rnds 2–8: Rep rnds 2–8 of First Leg.

WAIST TRIM

Working in starting ch on opposite side of rnd 1 on Bloomers, join lime berry with sc in first ch, sc in each ch around, join in beg sc. Fasten off.

Tie blue berry in bow around center front st below Waist Trim. ❑❑

Shawl

Design by Darla Hassell

SKILL LEVEL
■ ■ □ □
EASY

FINISHED SIZE
35 inches long x 70 inches wide

MATERIALS
- Red Heart LusterSheen fine (sport) weight yarn (4 oz/335 yds/113g per skein): 4 skeins #0517 turquoise
- Size E/4/3.50mm crochet hook or size needed to obtain gauge
- Size 35 broomstick lace needle

GAUGE
5 sts = 1 inch

INSTRUCTIONS

SHAWL

Row 1: Ch 277, dc in 4th ch from hook and in each ch across, turn. *(275 dc)*

Row 2: Ch 1, sc in first st, ch 5, sk next 4 sts, sc in next st, [ch 15, sk next 11 sts, sc in next st] 22 times, ch 5, sk next 4 sts, sc in last st, turn. *(22 ch-15 sps, 2 ch-5 sps)*

Row 3: Sl st in each of next 5 chs, sl st in next st, ch 1, 20 sc in each ch-15 sp across, leaving last ch-5 sp unworked, **do not turn.** *(440 sc)*

Row 4: Working left to right, slip last lp on hook onto broomstick, sk first st, [insert hook in next st, yo, pull lp through st and slip onto broomstick *(see Fig. 1)*] across, sk next 2 chs of next ch-5, sl st in next ch, **do not turn,** slip first 4 lps from broomstick onto hook, yo, pull lp through all 5 lps on hook *(see Fig. 2)*, ch 1, 5 sc in same 4-lp group *(see Fig. 3)*, ch 2, *[slip next 4 lps from broomstick onto hook, yo, pull lp through 4 lps on hook, yo, pull through 2 lps on hook *(sc made)*, 4 sc in same 4-lp group, ch 2] 3 times**, slip next 8 lps from broomstick onto hook, yo, pull through 8 lps on hook, yo, pull through 2 lps on hook *(sc made)*, 4 sc in same 8-lp group, ch 2, rep from * across, ending last rep at **, slip last 4 lps from broomstick onto hook, yo, pull lp through 4 lps on hook, yo, pull through 2 lps on hook *(sc made)*, 4 sc in same 4-lp group, dc in next ch-5 sp, turn. *(89 5-sc groups)*

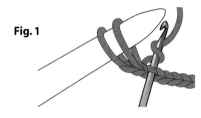

Fig. 1

Fig. 2

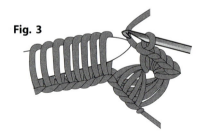

Fig. 3

Broomstick Lace

Row 5: Ch 1, sc in each of first 6 sts, ch 2, sk next ch sp, sc in each of next 5 sts, ch 2, sk next ch sp, sc in each of next 3 sts, [ch 10, sc in center st of next 5-sc group] 84 times, leaving rem sts unworked, turn. *(84 ch-10 sps)*

Rows 6 & 7: Ch 1, 5 sc in first ch sp, [ch 10, sc in next ch sp] across, turn. *(83 ch sps, 82 ch sps)*

Row 8: Ch 1, 9 sc in first ch sp, 4 sc in next ch sp, working left to right, slip last lp on hook onto broomstick, sk first st, [insert hook in next st, yo, pull lp through st and slip onto broomstick] 7 times, sl st in next sc, ch 4, slip 8 lps from broomstick onto hook, yo, pull lp through all 9 lps on hook, ch 1, 5 sc in same 8-lp group, ch 4, sc in same ch sp as last half of 8-lp broomstick lace st, *[ch 10, sc in next ch sp] 3 times, 4 sc in same ch sp as last sc, 4 sc in next ch sp, working left to right, slip last lp on hook onto broomstick, sk first st, [insert hook in next st, yo, pull lp through st and slip onto broomstick] 7 times, sl st in next sc, ch 4, slip 8 lps from broomstick onto hook, yo, pull lp through all 9 lps on hook, ch 1, 5 sc in same 8-lp group**, ch 4, sc in same ch sp as last half of 8-lp broomstick lace st, rep from * across, ending last rep at **, **dtr** *(see Stitch Guide)* in same ch sp as last half of 8-lp broomstick lace st, turn. *(60 ch sps, 21 5-sc groups)*

Row 9: Ch 1, sc in each of next 3 sc, [ch 10, sc in next ch sp or in center st of next 5-sc group] across, turn. *(80 ch sps)*

Rows 10 & 11: Ch 1, 5 sc in first ch sp, [ch 10, sc in next ch sp] across, turn. *(79 ch sps, 78 ch sps)*

Rows 12–44: Rep rows 8–11 consecutively, ending with row 8. Fasten off at end of last row.

Row 45: Join with sc in end of row 1, 2 sc in same row, ch 1, evenly sp [dc, ch 1] across ends of rows, working across last row, [dc, ch 1] across with (dc, ch 2, dc, ch 1) in center st of each 5-sc group and (dc, {ch 1, dc} twice, ch 2, dc, {ch 1, dc} twice, ch 1) in each ch-10 sp, working across ends of rows, evenly sp [dc, ch 1] across to row 1, 3 sc in end of row 1. Fasten off. ❑❑

Scarf

Design by Darla Hassell

SKILL LEVEL

EASY

FINISHED SIZE
90 inches long, not including Fringe

MATERIALS
- DMC Senso 100% Cotton size 3 crochet cotton (150 yds per ball):
   - 2 balls #1004 guava orange
   - 1 ball #1009 anise green
- Size 0/2.50 steel crochet hook
- Size E/4/3.5mm crochet hook or size needed to obtain gauge
- Size 19 knitting needle
- Tapestry needle
- 28 wooden 8mm beads

GAUGE
Size E hook: 2 sc and 2 ch-4 sps = 2 inches

SPECIAL STITCH
Cluster (cl): Yo twice, insert hook in designated ch, yo, pull lp through, [yo, pull through 2 lps on hook] twice, yo twice, insert hook in same ch, yo, pull lp through, [yo, pull through 2 lps on hook] twice, yo, pull through all 3 lps on hook.

INSTRUCTIONS
SCARF
Row 1: With size E hook and guava orange, ch 463, **do not turn,** slip last lp on hook onto knitting needle, working left to right, back towards slip knot, [insert hook in next ch, yo, pull lp through ch and slip onto needle *(see Fig. 1)*] 14 times, *with size 0 hook, pull end of ch through 1 bead, push bead up next to last lp, sk ch behind bead [insert hook in next ch, yo, pull lp through ch and slip onto needle] 15 times, rep from * across, **do not turn,** slip first 5 lps from needle onto hook, yo, pull lp through all 5 lps on hook *(see Fig. 2)*, ch 1, 5 sc *(see Fig. 3)* in same 5-lp group,

[ch 1, slip next 5 lps from needle onto hook, yo, pull lp through 5 lps on hook, yo, pull through 2 lps on hook *(sc made)*, 4 sc in same 5-lp group] across, ch 4, **cl** *(see Special Stitch)* in end ch, ch 4, cl in same ch, ch 4, **do not turn.** Fasten off. *(87 5-sc groups)*

Row 2: Working in starting ch on opposite side of row 1, starting on opposite end from last cl, working left to right, insert hook in first ch, pull up lp and slip onto knitting needle, skipping chs behind beads, [insert hook in next ch, yo, pull lp through ch and slip onto needle] across, **do not turn,** slip first 5 lps from needle onto hook, yo, pull lp through all 5 lps on hook, ch 1, 5 sc in same 5-lp group, [ch 1, slip next 5 lps from needle onto hook, yo, pull lp through 5 lps on hook, yo, pull through 2 lps on hook *(sc made)*, 4 sc in same 5-lp group] across, ch 4, (cl, ch 4, cl) in end ch, ch 4, join with sl st in next sc. Fasten off. Tack last ch-4 on row 1 to next sc.

Rnd 3: Now working in rnds, with size E hook and anise green, join with sc in 1 end ch-4 sp, (2 sc, ch 3, 3 sc) in same sp, ch 4, sc in next ch-4 sp, [ch 4, sc in center st of next 5-sc group] across, ch 4, sc in next ch-4 sp, ch 4, (3 sc, ch 3, 3 sc) in next end ch-4 sp, ch 4, sc in next ch-4 sp, [ch 4, sc in center st of next 5-sc group] across, ch 4, sc in next ch-4 sp, ch 4, join with sl st in beg sc. Fasten off.

FRINGE

For each Fringe, cut 14 strands guava orange, each 10 inches long. With all strands held tog, fold in half, insert hook in ch sp, pull fold through, pull all loose ends through fold. Tighten and trim ends.

Attach 1 Fringe to ch-3 sp on each end of Scarf. ❑❑

Fig. 1

Fig. 2

Broomstick Lace

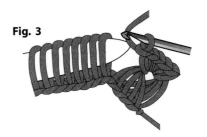

Fig. 3

306 East Parr Road
Berne, IN 46711
© 2006 Annie's Attic

TOLL-FREE ORDER LINE or to request a free catalog (800) LV-ANNIE (800) 582-6643
Customer Service (800) AT-ANNIE (800) 282-6643, **Fax** (800) 882-6643
Visit anniesatticcatalog.com

We have made every effort to ensure the accuracy and completeness of these instructions. We cannot, however, be responsible for human error, typographical mistakes or variations in individual work. Reprinting or duplicating the information, photographs or graphics in this publication by any means, including copy machine, computer scanning, digital photography, e-mail, personal Web site and fax, is illegal. Failure to abide by federal copyright laws may result in litigation and fines.

ISBN-10: 1-59635-139-X   ISBN-13: 978-1-59635-139-4

Stitch Guide

ABBREVIATIONS

beg	begin/beginning
bpdc	back post double crochet
bpsc	back post single crochet
bptr	back post treble crochet
CC	contrasting color
ch	chain stitch
ch-	refers to chain or space previously made (i.e., ch-1 space)
ch sp	chain space
cl	cluster
cm	centimeter(s)
dc	double crochet
dec	decrease/decreases/decreasing
dtr	double treble crochet
fpdc	front post double crochet
fpsc	front post single crochet
fptr	front post treble crochet
g	gram(s)
hdc	half double crochet
inc	increase/increases/increasing
lp(s)	loop(s)
MC	main color
mm	millimeter(s)
oz	ounce(s)
pc	popcorn
rem	remain/remaining
rep	repeat(s)
rnd(s)	round(s)
RS	right side
sc	single crochet
sk	skip(ped)
sl st	slip stitch
sp(s)	space(s)
st(s)	stitch(es)
tog	together
tr	treble crochet
trtr	triple treble
WS	wrong side
yd(s)	yard(s)
yo	yarn over

Chain—ch: Yo, pull through lp on hook.

Slip stitch—sl st: Insert hook in st, yo, pull through both lps on hook.

Single crochet—sc: Insert hook in st, yo, pull through st, yo, pull through both lps on hook.

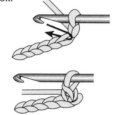

Front loop—front lp
Back loop—back lp

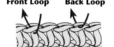

Front post stitch—fp:
Back post stitch—bp: When working post st, insert hook from right to left around post st on previous row.

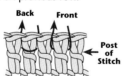

Half double crochet—hdc: Yo, insert hook in st, yo, pull through st, yo, pull through all 3 lps on hook.

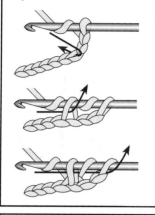

Double crochet—dc: Yo, insert hook in st, yo, pull through st, [yo, pull through 2 lps] twice.

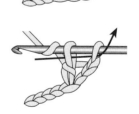

Change colors: Drop first color; with 2nd color, pull through last 2 lps of st.

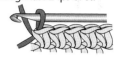

Treble crochet—tr: Yo 2 times, insert hook in st, yo, pull through st, [yo, pull through 2 lps] 3 times.

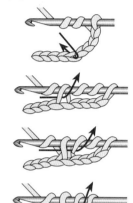

Double treble crochet—dtr: Yo 3 times, insert hook in st, yo, pull through st, [yo, pull through 2 lps] 4 times.

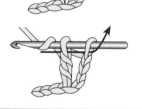

Single crochet decrease (sc dec): (Insert hook, yo, draw up a lp) in each of the sts indicated, yo, draw through all lps on hook.

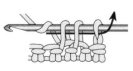
Example of 2-sc dec

Half double crochet decrease (hdc dec): (Yo, insert hook, yo, draw lp through) in each of the sts indicated, yo, draw through all lps on hook.

Example of 2-hdc dec

Double crochet decrease (dc dec): (Yo, insert hook, yo, draw lp through, yo, draw through 2 lps on hook) in each of the sts indicated, yo, draw through all lps on hook.

Example of 2-dc dec

Treble crochet decrease (tr dec): Holding back last lp of each st, tr in each of the sts indicated, yo, pull through all lps on hook.

Example of 2-tr dec

US		UK
sl st (slip stitch)	=	sc (single crochet)
sc (single crochet)	=	dc (double crochet)
hdc (half double crochet)	=	htr (half treble crochet)
dc (double crochet)	=	tr (treble crochet)
tr (treble crochet)	=	dtr (double treble crochet)
dtr (double treble crochet)	=	ttr (triple treble crochet)
skip	=	miss

For more complete information, visit
AnniesAttic.com